Shut Up and Text!

Your way to 100k

Kevin Marino

Table of Contents

Forward

My goal in the pages that follow is not just to tell people what they need to do, but to provide some background and theory as to why it works. There will be insights into why the vast majority of people struggle in their network marketing businesses and I'll also tell you what steps can be taken to guarantee better results. I have a very annoying habit of being able to point out the blatantly obvious in a way you may not have heard before, but which will now give you that "Ah ha!" moment.

What you will come to learn, is that I love to help people succeed but I do it a bit differently than most. I am going share EVERYTHING with you ... not necessarily what you WANT to hear but will tell you what you NEED to hear and yes, it will be done with my own typical, "in your face type of flare" because that's what I excel at. So, if you are good with me, "keeping it real," keep reading. You will have a blast and learn some amazing stuff! If that scares you, then put the book down now, step away, and give it to a friend who isn't afraid of the truth!

OK ... so you're still reading - and that makes you my type of person! One who didn't come here for some light entertainment ... you came here for grit, substance, detail and an action plan! Right! Ready? Then let's do this!

CHAPTER ONE

Who is This Spikey Hair Guy?

It's always good to know something about the guy who is, let's face it, giving you straight-from-the-hip advice on how to turn yourself into a money-making machine. After all, you probably never heard of me before today. So let me give you a bit of background on who I am and how going broke a few times (stop laughing) was an amazing learning experience and taught me that poor IS a state of mind and being 'broke' was just a temporary status.

Who I am? I am someone who has been an entrepreneur his entire life, a "serial entrepreneur," if that makes sense to you. As I went through school it was interesting. I had fun. I was a dedicated athlete and was very big on, "team." In fact, "team," has always been an intrinsic part of my whole being since I was six years old. I still play team sports to this day and it's still a big part of my life.

As a youngster I began mowing lawns, shovelling driveways, raking leaves, and doing other yard stuff. I didn't like doing it in my own yard of course, but if anyone in the neighbourhood needed work, and would part with a few bucks - I was there! Then, in high school there was lifeguarding (an awesome job hanging out in the sun and yelling at kids to behave and when they didn't, we made them pick weeds!). In the winter, using a friend's jeep, we would drive around in snowstorms and pull folks out of snow banks for a few bucks.

Rear wheel drive vehicles were terrible in the snow and turned out to be huge money makers for us!

Then I was off to college, and it was there I realized I really had a knack for this, "entrepreneur thing." Even though I was achieving very good grades and was cranking through my courses, I said to myself, "I do not want to sit in a cubicle or an office for the rest of my life." I was a computer science and math major and I quickly realized if I didn't change things, my future would be filled with just that ... cubicles and corporation offices. I decided I would actually prefer a stiff beating!

Understand, I was the guy on campus who had the red arm from stirring the grain punch! You know, when you used to make such a large batch of punch you had to do it in a large rubber trashcan ... YES ... in a 30-gallon drum! The largest party I mixed for required multiple batches and 16 litters of grain! Let me tell you, that served a small army. There were about 120 people that had slept over (passed out) in our dorm and yes, I counted them as I was checking out the common areas the next morning while eating the oranges that remained at the bottom of the punch bowl/can.

Now, here was the cool thing and I'm sure this is where some of you are wondering what all this has to do with being an entrepreneur. Well think about this ... I charged $5 per head to attend the parties I ran. I would pre sell to 50 plus people, which meant I covered the cost of the booze, lemons, oranges, Hawaiian Punch mix, ginger ale and orange soda (now you have my recipe), even before the party started. It would typically cost $200 - $300 for all the supplies and I always told people to bring chips and other snacks and of course their $5.

The most I ever netted in one party was over $1,400! Not bad for a poor, starving college kid. One monster party per semester and I covered most of my food bills. At that age in my life I ate everybody out of house and home. Yeah, at that age I ate more than some small villages and didn't gain much weight. In fact, I graduated high school the same height (5'11") I am now but weighing only 120 pounds. Yeah, I was 65 pounds lighter than I am right now and I am still not heavy.

So it was while attending college that I had one of those, AHA!, eye opening moments. The firm realization, before sliding further into debt, that I didn't want to be that person sitting at a computer in a cubical. As I said, I was a computer science and math major in the early 80's. I asked myself, "What does that spell?" Boring desk job sitting in a cube farm, and, I decided, that's not me! I am not that type of personality. My personality type is into parties and other fun things; someone who goes out and meets people - LOTS of people! To put it bluntly, I'm into making money, but I have to enjoy what I'm doing ... simply making money and having no fun is NO WAY to live!

There and then I decided I didn't want to do this anymore. I had been running parties and bartending, and I thought, well, parties are fun, bartending is fun, why not just buy a bar? I got together with some friends. Between us we scraped some funds together and with the help of our credit cards, we bought a bar. That eventually turned into four, three in Long Island and one in Connecticut.

CHAPTER TWO

The Difference

I realized at some point that I was different from most people ... I was an entrepreneur and folks who LIKE working in a cubicle simply didn't get me. You need to understand that if you are an entrepreneur many people, who prefer to be worker bees, will not understand you. They view entrepreneurs as odd or weird. Embrace that fact, because if you really do want to be an entrepreneur, a lot of people will look at you strangely your entire life. Why? Because we take chances, we do. Why do we take chances? Because we don't want to settle for what someone else wants to pay us! I have never settled for what somebody wants to pay me. Even when I did work for others, I always negotiated a bonus or percentage, because I always wanted to have a piece of the outcome from my hard work that went beyond the, "hourly wage." It's like when an entrepreneur is told to pick from options A or B, he says, "I don't like either ... let's invent option D!

You need to understand the job industry. An employer typically pays an employee just enough for them not to quit and the employee typically works just hard enough not to get fired. That's normal for most people because they have no interest in the business itself. Therefore, they're being paid to do their work. They are being paid to, "care," about somebody else's business. Does that make sense to you? Even if somebody is being paid to care, there is really no way they will care as much as if they owned the place.

One of the things I did when I owned businesses was I incentivized people. I used to tell my employees, "If you go above and beyond, then you will share in the profits of the business." Guess what happened? They cared more. Most of them watched my back. Why? Because they had an additional interest in the profitability of my business. They now viewed it as OUR business, which was a much better mindset for them, for the customers, for the partners and of course, for me.

It was in the early 90's, when I owned the bars and restaurants, that my network marketing career started. I found network marketing, or maybe it found me, whatever, it was something that really intrigued me. First up ... satellite dishes. Yes, my first network marketing experience was in selling satellite dishes. You know the DirecTV little dishes? Well, back then there was EchoStar and there was DirecTV. We hooked up with EchoStar and we had the network marketing exclusive for satellite dishes. Think about this: The dish cost $800 and another $200 to install it. What is it now? Yeah, FREE. Not a long-term, sustainable residual.

So I left that business and went into Telecoms. Do you remember when long distance calls used to cost 25 cents a minute? Youngsters probably get very confused by those figures, but that is what it was. I remember long ago gathering around the kitchen table. At that time my grandmother lived in Florida and we would call her every Sunday night because after 7:00pm on Sunday the call rates were lower. They dropped to 10 cents so we could call Florida for 60% less. We would pass the phone around and chat for about 30 minutes.

Some very interesting things happened to me after I started working in network marketing. First I struggled because, basically, I was a bit lazy. (Shh! Don't tell anyone). However, I finally smartened up and started paying attention to the big guns that were already making big money. I found a couple mentors and began buying all their VHS tapes and cassettes. (Hey, no old guy jokes!) I started to listen to what they and other leaders in the profession, were saying. It was amazing because they were all saying something similar ... just in different ways.

It occurred to me one day that I could do what they were doing ... BUT ... and it was one huge Everest-sized but ... I was scared to death of speaking in public! It was a hangover from school. Playing the class clown in the back of the room or playing baseball in front of a couple thousand people ... NO PROBLEM ... standing up in front of people and speaking? ARE YOU NUTS?!?

Nevertheless, I began implementing some of the great info I was learning from my mentors and other leaders. Success was starting to happen! And with that success came requests for me to assist on conference calls. I swallowed my fears and hosted some calls by welcoming people, bantering with them a bit and then introducing the featured speaker. Piece of cake! I started becoming comfortable with my new, upgraded role.

Then one day I was hosting the call and the featured speaker didn't show up! Wow, here was a gut check! What to do? I just assumed he would be there when I needed him to be. Then I thought maybe he was on mute ... yeah! That's it, he was on mute and would very soon realize and unmute. So I said, "Hey bud. Unmute your phone." Just then a message arrived at my desk (via another phone as there was no texting) saying the speaker had car trouble and was in a very bad cell area! UGH! I'm sure you can see where this is leading. I had two choices: 1. Apologize to the hundreds of eager people who were on the call and ask them to come back a few days later when the speaker would be there, or 2. Throw caution to the winds, use my crazy recall skills and have some fun!

You see, I was one of those kids that didn't have to study too hard in school. I really ticked off a lot of people because I could just sit and listen in class, absorbing everything I needed to, and then ace a test without notes, doing homework or studying. Math especially. I can listen to numbers and absorb them quickly. And I can pretty much regurgitate it all back. I came to find out that was a VERY useful skill in network marketing!

So Yeah, I picked 2. Mouth as dry as the Gobi desert, I threw all caution to the winds and plunged straight into my presentation. Was it great? ... NO! ... But I discovered folks liked my more, "human," or as some put it, "wise guy," approach to the call. I cracked a few jokes, stuttered, lost my train of thought multiple times, and turned a 20-minute presentation into well over 30 minutes because I wanted to be sure I covered everything. Then, just as I was closing out the call, I heard a voice I recognized! Seemed my leader had pulled a fast one on me! He had feigned a traffic delay to make me step up. He closed out the call by letting everyone know that it had been my first official presentation, which he had tricked me into doing on zero notice - and I had crushed it! Then he thanked me for filling in for him while he had, "car trouble." We all knew I hadn't, "crushed it," but the experience really pumped me up and gave me huge confidence to do it again. To the point in fact, where I ended up running five conference calls a day. Saying I had become comfortable in the role would be a slight understatement. I found I actually enjoyed it!

CHAPTER THREE

Stepping Up Again – And Again!

The next crazy stepping up I had to do in Network Marketing was about a year later at The Meadowlands Sheraton in NJ. I remember it well because the thing I feared most actually happened! It was an eastern regional meeting, well over 300 people in attendance, and the corporate trainers from Utah missed their connecting flight in St. Louis, so they were not going to land in time to do the Friday night overview presentation.

All the leaders gathered round. Concern clouded all their faces because the most amazing presenter I had ever seen was not going to make it and someone had to fill in. Like a fool I simply asked the question as to who that would be. They all turned and looked at me! (Stream of conscious thought) (UH … Hell NO! … I've never done this! Not just that … I DON'T speak in public! NO

... you can't be serious! ... Look at me shaking! ... it's 7:24pm and this thing is due to start at 7:30 ... ahhhh ... these people are nuts). Yes, ALL this went through my mind in about two seconds and I went pale!

One of the leaders looked at me and said, "You know the material the best, you've been doing the calls for a year ... just do it!"

Well who was I to argue with pure logic? It was that night in NJ in the mid-90's that forever changed my network marketing career. And it wasn't because I was great that night, I wasn't though I was pretty good for my first time. But, it was a major AHA! moment for me ... I was not afraid to speak in public any longer! What? Yeah, craziest thing - I just started having a conversation with the audience in my mind and then nature took over. A few jokes, some stuttering, some umms and uhhs, some William Shatner pregnant pauses, but it wasn't painful and I wasn't dying ... I was enjoying it!!!

I went on to do many presentations for that company and even became one of their national trainers ... yet another step up.

Then what happened to phone rates? They went down and down and down and down. And as they went down, so the margins went down. As a result, a lot of these companies were buying and selling each other. I was loving network marketing, but we were bouncing from one company to another because they kept buying and selling each other. The situation led to ever shrinking residual checks. It was time to move on.

I ventured into a product based nutrition company, which I am still a customer of to this day, and I still love their flagship product after almost 20 years. I also still receive a check from a company out of California although I have not put anything into it since the late 90's, that's true residual income! Personally, I'm not a big product seller ... but I buy TONS of it because I believe many of the top products in the world originate with network marketing companies.

As my career matured, I found myself working with companies I didn't enjoy working with. Yes, I was part of a team, but I just wasn't enjoying it and that, along with a lack of home front support, caused me to rethink my network marketing future. The money was decent, but I just wasn't having any fun! I needed fun!

If this happens to you when you are working in a job, you have a choice, you either quit and find another job, or you suck it up. Well, in a home-based business, if you find yourself working with people you don't want to work with, you also have a couple of choices, you can either quit or go build a new network in a new company.

At the time when I was not happy, someone approached me and tweaked my entrepreneurial juices by asking me to become part of a, "regular company." It was jewellery manufacturing. I looked right at the guy and I said, "All right. You want me to become a partner in this new jewellery manufacturing company. What does that have to do with anything I've ever done in my entire life?" He explained to me how the type of fine jewellery ring manufacturing we would be involved in was all math based! So, I thought about it. I'm a math guy, it's math based, it could be fun … okay I'm in.

Have you heard of zales.com? It's one of the largest jewellery retailers in the USA. There's a really cool feature on the website. If you go on to zales.com, you will find a "Design Your Own," section where you are able to pick the type of stone you want, the size of the ring, the total carat weight of the diamonds, the quality – everything, and it prices for you right there on the fly. The customer is given the exact pricing based on the actual cost of the raw materials that week. Sound cool? Yeah! Well, I did all the math behind that site. It's really cool! We used to make one-offs for Zales. We stored all the boxes and packing supplies for the company, they'd send us the order from the site, and we would manufacture and ship the product out, in about a week, directly to the person. The product was custom-made for them. It was an interesting time in my life, but I always felt something was missing. That business was eventually sold off and I went in search of my next project.

CHAPTER FOUR

Up, Down, Then Up, Up, Up!

I don't know what I was thinking, but being an entrepreneur I decided to go into high-end residential housing! I know … where's the continuity … where did that segue come from? I'm still not sure, but I knew I wanted something different and it had to be new, something I had never done before. I found a guy, or he found me.. not really sure how that worked but it did. He was looking for a project manager and I was looking for a home. He made me a very fair offer, (yes, an interest in the outcome was part of my bonus, together with a huge incentive!) and we went to work. So there we were, building three to six million dollar homes in Westport, Connecticut. It was very new and exciting and my math skills came in very handy.

Does anybody remember what happened in 2008 and 2009? Yeah, banks crashing, brokerages crashing, housing market destroyed for years! The business was shut down and as luck would have it, at the very same time all this joyous stuff was happening, I was going through a divorce and ended up, I believe the technical term is, "dead-ass broke," because there's broke and then there's the hole I found myself in. Ugly is just the beginning of the description of where I was. It was very, very ugly and it was the third time in my life I'd been broke and I'd done it differently each time ... stop laughing!

People used to come up to me during and after my ordeals and say, "Oh my, you're poor again."

My reply was always the same. "No, I'm broke. I'm not poor. Poor is a state of mind. I'm not poor - I just don't have any money at the moment. I've done it before I'll do it again."

"How?" They used to ask.

"I have no idea," I would reply. "But I will figure it out."

And I did!

I borrowed money against a life insurance policy I had had for years and built an apartment over my buddy's garage. I was refereeing three sports so I stayed in shape and I was, at least, making a little bit of money. But I had no concrete plans ...

Then somebody came to me one day and said, "Hey, can you do me a favor and give me your opinion on this business I am looking into?"

I started laughing. I said, "Really? You're going to drag me to a network marketing presentation?" Because we all know what he had said is code for come look at my business and hopefully join. We know what's it's code for because we've all said it, probably a hundred times, or even thousands of times.

I went down, well … actually at first I said, "No, I don't think so."

The person looked at me and said, "Here's the deal. You're broke, and I know you've done network marketing before, plus you used to be really, really good." I still find it difficult to believe he used LOGIC on me!

Anyway, I decided to go down and take a look. I reviewed the company, the products, and the compensation plan. It looked interesting so I signed up. I started working and I started making some extra money. This is what it's all about, right? It's about finding a business, plugging yourself in and starting to work.

Well, the math side of me kicked in, albeit a bit late and I started to do the math behind the company. I quickly realized they were in big trouble. I sat down with the president of the company and I said, "You're in big trouble this isn't going to work." And I went through the figures with him.

He listened, and then said, "Okay, I'll take it under advisement."

The cool thing was that I met a gentleman, during that period of time, who had sold off his energy business for about 50 million dollars a few years earlier. He was working in network marketing because he was bored and craved the social aspect of it. All very interesting, but here's how we really met. I was actually leaning on his car when he walked out and hit the unlock button, which gave out this tone that was somehow different. I jumped away and said, "Wow! That's a nice car!"

His response was classic, "It had better be - it's a Bentley!"

I kind of chuckled. I knew the guy had money, but I didn't know he was that well off. I mean I didn't know he had, "Bentley," money. I think we can agree that Bentley money was WAY better than Kevin money?

We got to know each other pretty well and a few months later he approached me. "Here's the deal," he said. "I'm going to start a company and I know you're broke. I like your personality. I'd like you to be part of that company."

I said, "I'm in.

He looked surprised. "Why did you jump so fast?"

I said, "Are you kidding me? My mamma did not raise a fool."

There was a guy who had just sold his company for 50 million dollars, and he's starting a new company. I didn't care what he was selling ... I was IN! His train was in motion again, and I was hooking my Kaboose … (don't tell me it's spelled wrong)… to it! It means Kevin's caboose … and I hooked it to that energy train. I didn't care that the track had not even been laid … I didn't care that there was no executive staff … no concrete business plan. Why didn't I care? Because I AM AN ENTREPRENEUR! Many people told me I was nuts, and that was totally fine with me, as I have heard that most of my life.

So I jumped aboard. I hooked my kaboose to that train, and off we went for an amazing ride in the energy field. The first nine months were terrible; I mean they were *really* terrible. I worked my tail off and built teams of people. We were a direct selling company. We went and knocked on doors. It was awful, knocking on doors in good weather and the worst of weather. And I taught other people how to do the same. It was horrible, and I made just under $17,000 in that nine-month period.

We sat down at the end of that year and I told the owner, rather bluntly, "This sucks." He always liked me because I'm very direct. If there's one thing a lot of people learn pretty quickly about me it's that I'm pretty direct. I don't do it in a mean way, I try to do it in a constructive way but, occasionally, I need to get someone's attention.

I explained the issues to him. Fortunately, about that time, other people were starting to realize we needed help too. Consultants were brought in and the company switched tracks within about a three-month period of time. We totally relaunched as a network marketing company. I lost over 90% of my organization when that happened, but those that stayed saw the power (no pun intended) of the new plan and direction. In fact, by the end of that year, I was earning well over $17,000 per month - the difference between knocking on doors and building networking teams. Building networking teams, and teaching them to do the same thing you do, is how to make serious money. It's called leverage!

With the remaining 150 – 200 reps, we went on to build a team in excess of 146,000 in 3½ years and I became a seven figure earner. Now, I had decent results in the 90's, and in the early 2000's, but I had never achieved those kinds of results. I didn't do it by sponsoring 5,000 people. We sponsored less than 300 hundred and of those 300, about 165 actually did some work. Of those 165, about 60 were pretty good, 18 were really good, and seven were AWESOME! Those seven people were just driven, focused people who we worked very closely with. We taught them to teach others and those others taught others and so on. After a while, the field generals we had created did the same and then they created generals, and then they created generals, and then … well, you get the picture.

CHAPTER FIVE

Real Freedom And A Book To Read

What did that accomplish? People will tell you it's about financial freedom, did you ever hear of that? It's all about financial freedom. Financial freedom is important, but what many people don't realize is that what financial freedom really buys is TIME freedom - if you do network marketing properly.

I know a number of people who have a lot of money and have zero time. Anybody know a really good doctor, lawyer or business owner? They don't have any time. I have an optometrist friend, he makes awesome money. When his family goes away on vacation for three weeks, he joins them for most of the last week. How ridiculous is that? That's not what is supposed to happen. Going out and earning money, even making a boatload of the stuff is great, but not if it consumes your entire life and takes you away from the things that are important to you.

What network marketing allows us to do is work with people, create teams, create leverage and if you teach and train all your team members correctly, they will duplicate what you do. If you teach them to teach correctly, they duplicate again. Understand, if you do this properly the larger your organization gets, the less you hear of problems - because they never make it to you. They are handled way before they get to you. If you create generals and then help them to create generals and help them create generals, understand it stops at the last general. And you know what we tell them? Go and create some of your own generals, so you don't have to deal with any issues either and then come hang with us on the beach.

One of my favorite books, when I made my comeback in network marketing and became a leader and a trainer, was the book, *Beach Money* , by Jordan Adler. I was sitting there and I looked at the book and I said, "You know what? That book is just calling my name." So I bought it. I read it and I said, "This guy knows me."

If you guys haven't come across Jordan Adler and you haven't read his book do yourself a favor read it, because it's about how to create a residual income, a situation where even if you go and lay on the beach, guess what shows up? You guessed it … money shows up. It might be in your mailbox or in your bank account, it doesn't matter which. Over the last few years, I've not only met Jordan but I have become friends with him. He's a great guy and I told him that *Beach Money* is one of the things that got me to focus on network marketing and commit to becoming a top leader and a trainer again. He asked me what I connected with so strongly. I told him that to me it all simply made sense! The power of network marketing, done properly, would allow me more time on the beach enjoying residual income. Again, someone was using logic on me!

CHAPTER SIX

Mentor Magic

OK, so if you are going to do this, let's do it right! If I'm going to do anything, I get in it to win it. But keep in mind, I don't like working "extra" for no reason. My goal is to figure out the most efficient way to do something, get the best results and then do that over and over and then teach that over and over!

All right, so what I have developed over the last couple of years is a system that anybody can follow and here's why I developed it. The most beautiful thing about this profession is, it's a people business. And the thing that will drive you the craziest about this profession is that it's a people business! People don't always follow instructions, because they typically believe they know how to do it better than you, even on their first day!

Have you ever known people who get started and they go out and they talk to everybody they know? Right out of the gate. You've warned them, "Don't say anything yet. We're going to be training on Saturday."

But this is only Tuesday so Wednesday, Thursday and Friday, they've spent talking to everyone they know and they don't want to go to training on Saturday because everybody said, "It's a scam."

Am I the only one this has happened to? People can't help themselves. They are excited, jazzed, and ready to take on the world and they want everyone to know right now!

- Do they understand the company yet? No

- Do they understand the compensation plan? No

- Do they know where to find all the tools? No

- Do they have a story, or know the story of some of the top leaders in the company yet? No

- Do they understand the products fully? No

- Do they know where to get all the answers? No

- Have they been to a training? No

- Have they written out their goals? No

- Have they started a vision board? No

- Have they put together a list? No

- Do they have a list of team leaders? No

- Do most even realize they have embarked on a brand-new profession? No I mean, come on people!

So, after getting so annoyed at people but then realizing I was also once one of "those" people who ran around and talked to everybody, I learned to keep my mouth shut. Let me tell you, keeping my mouth shut when someone was trying to teach me how to do this business was painful. However, having been a team sports guy my entire life, I realized that having a coach would shorten the learning curve for me. That was the reason I chose a mentor who was successful in this biz and we went to work. But he had the nerve to tell me that he wanted me to stop talking to people! At least that's the way I heard it. He was very successful, and I wanted to be that successful too, sooooo he gave me a two-minute egg timer. He said "When you make an approach phone call, when that thing stops you hang up. I don't care if you're mid-sentence. If you don't do that I'm not working with you."

OUCH! That was tough but he was someone who knew more than me and I needed to learn. If you don't find a coach or mentor, you won't grow, or if you do grow, it'll take you much longer to hit the top ranks. I am not into doing anything the long way when it comes to success. Teach it to me. I want to know. I want the shortcut. Why? Isn't it obvious by now? Because I want to go lie on the beach. I am extremely motivated to be lazy. Does that make sense? I will work my tail off so I can go and do nothing because folks, when I unplug, I unplug. I'm on a beach, people are bringing me drinks and I don't want to know from the world. Time freedom is what's it's all about.

CHAPTER SEVEN

Just Shut Up!

I don't know what you like to do …

- Maybe you like to ski.

- Maybe you like to scuba dive.

- Maybe you like to go on cruises.

- Maybe you want to tour Europe.

- Maybe you want to spend more time with your family.

- Maybe you want be there when your children get off the bus!

- Maybe you want to hang out on the beach with me. ☺

- Maybe you want to sculpt your shrubbery!

Whatever your 'like' is, if you had all the money you wanted, what would you do? Write it down. Here's the question again: If money was no object what would you do? Now understand, just because money is no object doesn't meantime isn't. If I can show you how to make the money and have more time, what would that be worth to you? We'll delve more into that shortly.

Back to what frustrating newbies do when they come into the business. I'm talking newbies for the moment, but you should all realize that I don't care how many years you've been doing this, you probably go around talking far too much. I call that verbally vomiting on people. Ugly thought, huh? All right, get that mental image, that is what you are doing and even if you don't realize that's what you're doing, it will certainly be how your prospects feel! Understand, it's not about what you think you're doing, it's about what's perceived from the other side.

If you approach someone with your business and sound like this:

"Oh my gosh! Xavier you got to see this thing, it is the greatest business in the world. You know, I've never been in my own business before and that is because I was waiting for this business to be invented! I mean when you see the product ... wow, it just blows you away and it may actually

provide you with better gas mileage, cure cancer or acne or something ... it's very versatile! Also, you won't believe how we get paid. It's a back office pay card/eWallet/OMGCoin thingy and you get paid daily, weekly or was it hourly ... like anyway, the money is awesome even though I'm not sure just how that works. You need to join right now and this way we can call everyone that you know right now, so you can get them before all the other people do!"

Your prospect will be looking at you like you are nuts. And can you blame him? You sound nuts! All your prospect wants to do is run the other way. But the fact remains, that's what many of you are currently doing without even realizing it. Maybe some of you do realize it, but you do it anyway, which is even crazier!

Back to my new egg timer. I had two minutes and I had to complete my mission of making a simple approach and hang up. It was difficult at first, but guess what? Eventually I was able to do it. I would write out my approach, and then trim it by keeping only info that was really necessary. It was amazing how fast two minutes went by and I felt like a crazy speed talker at times. Little by little it got easier ... my approach kept getting shorter until it was WELL under the two-minute limit I had been given in fact! This is what I learned along that journey.

It worked! Because … and here comes the, "magic sauce," **the less you say, the more money you make**. I know, it sounds crazy but it is downright true. The less you say, the more money you make. Or, maybe more importantly, the less you say to more people, the more money you make! If you stop yammering on at every single person, you will be able to approach many, many more!

CHAPTER EIGHT

Where Did This Texting Thing Come From?

Okay, that's enough about the trials and tribulations of my learning curve over the years! Let's now fast forward ... to early 2014. I had started noticing some disturbing, yet very interesting, trends. Most people hated picking up the phone to prospect people. Even the reps that didn't mind doing it, because they had been doing it for years, were getting poorer results and it was taking longer to build resulting in the feelings of frustration. The majority of people don't answer calls now because they know who is calling. They are busy and plan on calling you back later, which may or may not ever actually happen, so you call again and end up leaving another message. Again, an awful lot of people don't even listen to their voicemails!

The email side of the equation was even worse. Emails are rarely opened anymore because of the immense amount of spam and anyway folks can preview and delete without really reading the substance of the email. This trend is only worsening!

But get this, text messages were being opened within 12 minutes of receipt over 90% of the time, Whoa! Big, big question! How do we take advantage of that and other social media trends to begin a conversation and make a safe approach without being salesy?

How do we get people to just Shut Up and Text?

When I noticed this trend in 2014, nobody was using texting to prospect people or they were just crushing them on text, trying to sell them. One weekend I was doing a training RI with a guy that many of you probably have heard of. His name is Tom but he is known better as, "Big Al." He has written some amazing books! My absolute favorite is *The Four Color Personalities for MLM*. If you haven't read it, then read it. Read that book after you have finished this one! You will find it is the best way for you to understand who people are and how to speak to them, because people hear things in different ways according to their type of personality. I'm not going to go into it here because the book is an awesome read!

As Tom and I were sitting and chatting prior to our training, I said "Here's my idea but I'm having trouble with the script. I'm working on a quick, simple method of texting to get people's attention and begin a conversation. I love your wording, the way you put things because you really tweak people! I love that! My goal is to really just grab someone's attention ... not sell them. Would you mind helping me with some of the verbiage?" Being the giving guy that he is Tom readily agreed and we began to brainstorm.

We came up with a texting series where you don't speak to your prospect until they have responded to you at least twice. They have demonstrated an interest in the information, they have reviewed a video and are expecting your call! This process also cuts out up to 90% of the negativity associated with starting your network marketing business!

How's that for efficient?

As our team was building, we rolled out this new method of contacting prospects - and our business simply blew up even faster than it already was! We grew our team to over 146,000! It wasn't all with texting but it sure took all the pressure off the new recruits, got them growing and increased production - IMMEDIATELY!

How would you like to have a brand new recruit productive within a day? You see, if you teach them properly from day one to

"Be New" and make them understand that it isn't their job to know the answers ... it isn't their job to talk to everyone they run into ... it isn't their job to go on endlessly about their new business. Their ONE and ONLY job is to tee up prospects for the team leaders! That's it!!

WOW!!! Do you see how that will multiply?

CHAPTER NINE

Being New Is A Bonus

Think about this ... When does training begin? You see, most people think that training begins *after* a prospect signs up and begins reviewing videos in the back office; tuning into conference calls; attending local or regional trainings ... NOT!!! Training begins from the VERY first contact you have with a prospect. It includes things like:

- How you look.

- How you talk.

- How you carry yourself.

- What exactly you say?

- How you say it.

- Are you trying to sell them?

- Are you trying to recruit them, or GET them?

- Do you look or sound desperate?

With all this in mind, there are so many negative traps a new rep can fall into, any of which could turn a prospect off, which means the new rep kicks off their business on a negative note. This could easily sour the experience for some new folks and even scare them out of your business before they really get started. BUT, if you understand the job of the person who is prospecting is NOT to recruit or to sell or to talk on and on and on and on and on ... then you get the point. Their job is simply to keep putting the prospects in front of the team leaders ... the, "closers," ... the experts who can address the prospects' questions with the proper answers, and bring them closer to joining your business.

If you remember to "be new," ... I don't care if you have been in the company for years and know every single answer, if you personally answer questions put to you by YOUR prospects, then you are teaching them the wrong way to do the business from the moment you contacted them. In turn, their perception is that they must learn all the information you have discussed with them and probably more, so they will be able to answer all the questions that might come up when they begin talking to *their* prospects. If you close the deal, it follows that they will think they must close all their prospects. Most people don't like selling and that will be exactly what they are feeling. To most people, looking at possibly starting their own business this is a turn off. They have been told that network marketing is simple and already it is looking extremely complicated!

If the first contact is done properly, your prospect will realize they can succeed in this business. They will see that you simply sent them a few texts, shared a video or two, asked them a couple of quick questions and did a three-way with them and your team leader. Wow, they just realized that YOU didn't have to know a thing!! If this process is carried out properly, the prospect will realize that they *can* do this!

CHAPTER TEN

First Contact And How It Has Changed

L et's talk about first contact. Years ago, we had no choice but to call everyone on our lists. It was a long and tedious process but it was the only way. We would sit with our new rep ... work on their list, and begin the calling process. This was PAINFUL for many new prospects! We often ran into negative people (no, seriously, some people do have a negative outlook on life) and it would blow our new person right out of the game. If they survived and started to grow, many were not able to duplicate this process with their new prospects and it would fall to the team leaders to work with almost every new rep if there was to be any chance of duplication.

Today we have cell phones, but a lot of folks don't answer them. Fewer listen to their messages and still fewer return your calls! We also have email which has a less than 12% open rate ...

so good luck getting a response there too! The crazy thing is people are still communicating with each other. You just have to figure out where and what method yields the best open rate or response rate. The main question we need to answer is, "What is the most efficient way to begin a conversation?"

At this time, the top communication tool everyone looks at is texting! (And yes, FB Messenger also falls into this category). Yeah, everyone looks at their texts and I mean everyone! Think about this; you know that little red dot that appears over your messaging app on your phone and it has a little white number inside? When you see that do you open your texting or messaging app to see who is reaching out? Of course you do! Guess what? So does every single other person you know!! People won't always respond, but you know without a doubt … they read your message!

CHAPTER ELEVEN

So Are You Coachable And Can You Zip It?

I mean it. You are going to learn an incredible method of removing 90% or more of the negativity you typically run into when starting your business or bringing your networking business to the next level ... but you MUST be coachable!

I've asked many people if they are interested in making six or seven figures. Many say yes - and yet don't listen. When you are with someone who has been there and done it multiple times, and is willing to help you learn a process which absolutely works ... you have a choice: Do it your own way and keep struggling with duplication or go all in and fully commit to doing what has been proven to actually work in many different companies! That's right! I don't care what your network marketing company is selling or offering; benefits, products, energy, weight loss, water, energy drinks, discount buying, etc, etc. Get it?

First, I want to share the secret to building a monster organization: … Shut up!!

That is the single, biggest thing almost every network marketer needs help with. I was the worst when I started … ok … maybe not the worst, but I was in the top ten - along with a number of you who are currently reading this!

Remember, and I urge you to write this down, the more you say – the less you earn! The MORE you say – the LESS you EARN! repeat this over and over to yourself, it will help you do the first exercise - which is to **SHUT UP** ! (When prospecting).

You will soon realize that the secret to your new found success will be to say very VERY little to many, MANY people!

CHAPTER TWELVE

A Guarantee, Steps To Success, and How To Set Real Goals

L et's go through the steps that will GUARANTEE your success. Yes, I did say guarantee, because if you follow these steps, it is practically impossible to not succeed.

Whether you are new to your company or you are looking to bust through a plateau or you simply want to supercharge your growth, here are the steps you should absolutely take:

1. **Goals** – start by writing them down. Put some thought into them. You should be able to do this in a few hours. You will need one week, 30 day, 60 day, 90 day, six month, one year, 18 month, two year, three year, and five year goals. Having no goals is like leaving your house and getting in your car with no destination in mind. You're driving around and you look like

progress is being made, but you really aren't sure because there is no end destination.

If, on the other hand you leave your house and are headed four states over for a vacation and you have set a couple points along the way, to stop and eat and sleep for the night, you have a plan, you have weigh points. You have a clear destination which can be measured and if you are falling behind or take a wrong turn, you can see that, make corrections and get back on track.

It's exactly the same thing with your goals!

Also, the goals of those on your team should become very important to you. Simply put … if you help your team hit their goals … you will hit yours without even being focused on them.

2. **Vision Board** – I know you will hear people saying that it's a waste of time and make some whiny excuse why they don't have one. I don't care what anyone else's opinion is … do it! Why? Just one very good reason: Because it works!

Take a good size corkboard or poster board and tack your current goals in the center. Build your vision around it. Pictures, words, numbers, pages from magazines, real estate books, car ads, travel brochures, include kids, college, what will you do for yourself, what will you do for others … make a collage that means something to YOU!

Now the hard part! Come up with a hash tag (e.g. #MyName Vision Board). Share it with your family, your friends, your children, your team leaders, your team as you help them build theirs. Share it on social media. Tag any and all people online who are your supporters and your antagonists - tag them ALL!!

This process creates a self-made peer pressure group which will seriously assist you towards achieving your success as well as that of your team! You will come to a decision at some point, that you will not allow those people you have tagged to see you fail! It will push you to focus and strive for that which you have posted in the center of your Vision Board ... **YOUR GOALS!**

Very little helps a team member succeed faster than peer pressure! The more you share your Vision Board ... the MORE successful you will be.

3. This is the all-important ... **LIST!!!**

Think of your list of names as the retail product for your business. If you have no product to sell ... you have no business. If you have very little product, and never replace it ... you will have very little business and it won't grow. Therefore, you will not be successful.

So, how do you effectively write a list? Simple! Every name you put on that list is potentially worth $1,000! How much do you want to make? How willing are you to buckle down and sit with your phone and your social media contacts in front of you and start writing a REAL list. Grab a spiral notebook. (I said spiral for a reason so stop whining!) It is simply easier to work with than a legal style pad, so do it. (You are coachable ... remember!)

Now begin writing names. One name on every other line with a notation of where the lead has come from so you know where their contact info is located. When it's their turn to be contacted, you know exactly where to look. We only want the names on paper ...

Who do I include?

- Family

- Friends

- Acquaintances

- Co-workers

- Government workers

- People you meet in places you frequent

- People you like

- People you don't like. (You don't have to prospect them but you need to write them on the list because their names may

trigger the names of other people you know through them …
and you may actually like that other person!)

- People you meet in your everyday travels

- People from networking groups

- FaceBook

- LinkedIn

- Twitter

- Instagram

- Snapchat

Or any of the many social media platforms.

The AVERAGE person can come up with about 100-150
names. With some incentive, that same person will double or even
triple that list. If you have read this far, you are ABOVE average
and I expect you to do far better than the average person, so let's
see 400-500 to start! Remember, each name is potentially worth
$1,000, so how many will YOU start with? As I said, some of you
will double or triple that number! All adding to your potential
success story!

4. **Team Leaders** – You need a list including cell phone
   numbers of at LEAST four to six team leaders. This is crucial

to your success! This is **YOUR** success team! If your sponsor is new ... keep climbing. If their sponsor is new ... keep climbing! You need to find solid leaders who know the answers to the questions that your prospects are going to ask. Call each one of them and learn who they are. Learn their STORY ... what they've done, why they are here in this company, what successes they have experienced and what failures. Find out what industries they have worked in; real estate, construction, restaurants, office based, have they owned a traditional business, etc. You want to create a bio on each leader for a couple reasons: First, it is good that you get to know each other since you will be bringing them many prospects. Second, how can you introduce them to your prospects if you don't know who they are?

Don't let insecure sponsors or team leaders stop you from putting this list together. This is imperative to your future success. Explain to anyone giving you a problem, that you will be putting a lot of people on three-way calls and since one person will never always be available, you are looking for at least four to six contacts you can reach out to at a moment's notice.

If that reasoning doesn't work, just tell them Kevin Marino said it is imperative to my future success - so just give me the information! ☺

5. **Set Your Script** ! If your team leaders already have a Shut Up and Text script ready to go - great! If not, then look at some of the examples and adjust one slightly for your business. Most network marketing businesses will need a very slight tweak to make the script work for them.

Once you have it tweaked and are ready to go, make sure you have it available for your team to use as you begin to grow. At first you can share a word file, but you will want to set it up so the team can download from a central source, so if you need to make an adjustment at some point you will only need to make an announcement. This way everyone can simply get the new download which will have the newest version at

www.(yourcompany)textingscript.com

CHAPTER THIRTEEN

You Are Ready To Begin. Let's Do This!

O K ... you have a list! Now your job is to cross off as many names as possible from that list! How and why do you cross off a name? Well, the first few are easy; remember those people you put on the list that you don't like or would never want to work with ... yeah, them! If you followed instructions earlier, you have a bunch of those annoying people. CROSS THEM OUT! Enjoy doing it. Write a big "NOT" right next to their names! See, this is going to be FUN!!!

Now, a very important thing to remember; you will hear many people tell you that the money is in the follow up. Well, I told you at the beginning of this book I'm going to keep it very real with you ... this is a no BS zone!

The Money is in the DECISION!

And that is whether you are continually following up with a prospect for a month, two months, six months, a year, many years - you get my point! You are NOT making money! Am I saying don't do follow up ... NO ... I'm saying that you need to move your prospects toward a **DECISION.**

"Give me a YES or give me a NO ... I've got to go!"

A friend of mine has this pinned over his computer to remind him that it is NOT in his best interest to keep the conversation going with indecisive people for too long. I will share with you a bit later on what to do with those prospects who say, "No," and why leaders don't care if the answer is, "Yes," or, "No." They just want a DECISION!

Repeat this to yourself ... write it down where you can see it and live by it ... ***"The MONEY is in the DECISION!"***

CHAPTER FOURTEEN

OK, Let's Start Your Prospecting!

It's important to understand some of the psychology behind the wording. Your wording is important because you can REPEL people, based on your choice of words, or ATTRACT people based on your choice of words. Which would you prefer? Right! ... ATTRACT! Let's break this down!

Begin with blocks of 30 – 50 prospects. Send them a text. The first part of the text **MUST** grab their attention so wording is vital...

Hey John, I just found out ...

Hey John, I'm just curious ...

"I just found out ..." is a key phrase that tweaks the human brain. People want to know WHAT you just found out! If you want to test it with live subjects and have a bit of fun, try saying, "Hey, I just found out ...!" to your kids, your family, your friends, even someone you meet while you are out. Say, "Hey, I just found out …!" Then act a bit distracted and walk away! It's hilarious!

I challenge every single one of you to do this ASAP. Just look at someone and say, "Hey, I just found out …!" Then act a bit distracted and walk away. It will absolutely drive them crazy. Do it to your kids - they'll go nuts. You found out what? What? What? What? They're following you down the hall, what? Do it as research. It will give you huge confidence in the system you are getting ready to implement.

Another option which is also extremely effective, is the beginning *"Hey John, I'm just curious …"* Again, try this out on people, I highly suggest testing this on your spouse or significant other. This one also, works well on close friends and family. The reason it works so well is that people realize this opening usually leads to a question about something you want THEIR opinion on! People LOVE to give you their opinion - whether you want it or not. That makes it a great attention grabbing opening!

Now, what is the second part of the phrase? This also needs to be something attention grabbing but not salesy, so the person is inclined to respond to get more information on what you are talking about.

- What do you have to offer?

- What is your deal?

- What will grab people's attention?

- What do they need?

- How will what you have make their life better?

- How will it improve their situation?

- How will it be an answer to their need?

"Hey Mary, I just found out …"

- How we can get our electricity for free.

- How we can lose weight without starving.

- How we can get paid to get in shape.

- How we can take an extra vacation this year for free.

- How we can get cash back on our gas and groceries.

- How we can lose weight by drinking our morning coffee.

- How we can get healthier and be around for our grandkids.

- How we can stop having other people raise our kids.

- How we can be home every day as our kids get off the bus.

- How we can grow our husband's hair back. (LOL)

- How we can …

Notice the second part of the text is an inclusive statement which should pique their interest. Using the words, "we," and, "our," is inclusive. You're not attempting to SELL them anything. You are sharing information that will be of benefit to both of you. On the other hand, if you sent …

"Hey Mary, I just found out …"

- How you can get your electricity for free.

- How you can lose weight without starving.

- How you can get paid to get in shape.

- How you can take an extra vacation this year for free.

- How you can get cash back on your gas and groceries.

- How you can lose weight by drinking your morning coffee.

- How you can get healthier & be around for your grandkids.

- How you can stop having other people raise your kids.

- How you can be home every day as your kids get off the bus.

- How you can …

These phrases have a salesy feeling to them. To the reader it may feel as if you're talking at them and that you are about to try and sell them something. They are dreading the next text you send! Often, we are completely unaware of how our words are read by others … it's time to pay attention! The more attractive your words are, naturally, the more conversations you will be able to begin.

CHAPTER FIFTEEN

Sending Out That First Batch of Texts

This is going to be a long chapter, but all of it is good stuff – and vital to your success – please don't skip any part of it!

Most of you will be doing this via your phone but some will be using a texting or messaging program from your computer. ALWAYS, and I mean *always*, send the texts as individual messages ... NOT group messages! If you send a generic style message to 20 people at the same time, they will know you are ONLY trying to sell them something and really don't care about their individual situation.

I suggest typing your text out without personalizing it, then hit copy. This way you only need to hit paste, personalize it, and hit send for the next person. But be careful not to copy one you have already personalized or you may do what I did ... I typed it out ...

"Hey Julie, I just found out …"

Then I proceeded to hit paste and sent it to 50 individual people, completely forgetting to personalize it for each person! UGH! Yes, I sent, "Hey Julie," to at least 50 people! Needless to say, they were NOT all named Julie and I received some very interesting return texts! So please, always copy a NON-personalized text.

Keep a pen handy because you will need to notate the date and time for each person you text. In your spiral LIST notebook, where you left an open line between each name, you will be making a few notations and you need to be able to read them.

For example:

Joe Smith – T1 (4/15 @ 2:30pm)

Mary Jo – T1 (4/15 @ 2:30pm) – T2 (4/15 @ 2:45)

~~Chucky Jones~~ – NOT

Bobby D – T1 (4/15 @ 2:30pm)

Ira Goldberg – T1 (4/15 @ 2:30pm)

Bill Smith – T1 (4/15 @ 2:30pm) … SR … (means - snarky response)

This gives you an example of what your list will look like. Only yours, like mine, will be FAR messier than the one above. Make sure to leave a space between names so it will be easier for you to keep track of what phase each name is at. You'll notice above, we have a few things happening:

Chucky who we put on our list but don't want to work with. Joe, Bobby, Ira ... no response yet. Mary Jo we have sent text two. Bill has sent a snarky response ... I will deal with that shortly.

Now that your first batch of texts have been sent, you will soon realize there are now four possibilities.

1. The person ignores you.

2. The person sends you a snarky comment.

3. They respond inquisitively or positively.

4. They call you instead of texting.

This is where we get to cut out about 90% of the negativity - because of how they respond to your Text #1.

1. Let me first address the person who ignores you. You need to fully understand that THEY RECEIVED AND READ YOUR TEXT! Many times, people try to make excuses about what might be happening in their friend's life and why they

may have not seen their text or that it, perhaps may not have arrived ... NOT!

This is a no BS zone! They got it! To prove this fact to you, please think about when you receive a text message on your phone. On the top right of your little message icon appears red circle with a number in it ... Yes, or Yes? Ok. Is there any chance you will not look at that message at some point that day? Of course not! It's addictive and we ALL look at our texts. We may not respond to every single one - but we look at ALL of them!

So now you can understand that anyone who does not respond to you is doing so on purpose. I need you to be OK with that. We all have bad days or busy days when it just doesn't fit into our schedule to begin what might be a conversation with someone. Whether it's because it isn't a good time or the mood is just not right ... who knows ... maybe it's just been a terrible day ... whatever the reason for them not responding to you - *it doesn't matter* ... LET IT GO! I'll show you how to deal with that a bit later. For now, they have ignored you. YOUR RESPONSE IS TO IGNORE THEM TOO!

2. The next type of person you will deal with is Mr or Mrs Snarky Snark! These are the people who feel obliged to send you a rude, condescending or obnoxious return text!

- What are you doing now?

- You still selling that pond scum?

- Your electricity free yet?

- Are you going to live to be 124?

- Did your hair grow back?

- You buying an island yet?

- Is it one of those pyramid things?

- What's it going to cost me?

- I'm not doing meetings!

- Just send me your info I'll look at it one day ...

- Blah ... blah ... blah! (yes, I've gotten this one!)

The NERVE of them! That's it ... time to set them straight right? ... Well ... NO!!!! You are going to IGNORE them. I know you will want to get into a texting war with that person to show them how wrong they are and how right you are, but all that will accomplish is you alienating them for the future. Don't do it! Trust me on this! You must resist!

I've gotten into those texting wars myself, and, yes, I proved just how right I was, but in doing so, I figuratively chopped off my prospect's head! Yes, I was right! The only issue was that being right and proving it, made me zero dollars. And as a bonus, that person never wanted to hear from me about that or any other opportunity, ever again

Imagine for a minute, the person who sent you a snarky response might simply be having a terrible day. Something could have happened in their family and they could be stressed out. The family pet could be sick; they might have a hangnail and be all bent out of shape because of it … doesn't matter what the reason is … ignore them for now!

Remember, your goal is to avoid 90% of the negativity as you are beginning your business. That means you are dealing ONLY with those who respond positively to your first text. You may receive some snarky messages, but you will also receive some positive responses and they are easy to recognize:

- How? (Number one answer)

- Yes

- Tell me more

- What are you talking about?

- Ok, I'll bite

- Sounds interesting

- Cool ... send me details

- Sure

You will usually know when someone is being sincere, though occasionally one of your prospects will disguise their original answer and the follow up response will be snarky. You ignore them from that point on.

It is important you realize that nothing annoys a person, who is trying to get inside your head and put you off your game, more than you ignoring them. Treat it like a game, a serious game that YOU need to win and you don't win if you allow them to get in your head. If you allow them to do that - they win! Why? Because you have been distracted and are wasting time with someone who is clearly not ready to listen to you anyway. Again, I'll show you how to deal with them a couple of weeks later, it will be fun ... I promise!

3. Let's get to the positive responders! These are your golden prospects. Follow the script! Don't deviate:

- How? (Number one answer)

- Yes

- Tell me more

- What are you talking about?

- Ok, I'll bite

- Sounds interesting

- Cool ... send me details

- Sure

4. If the prospect calls you back ... **DO NOT ANSWER!** You hit the ignore button and treat them as a positive response, with the addition of, *"Sorry, I'm unable to talk at the moment ... but I have a very short video ... can you watch it right now?"*

Depending on how the prospect responds to this text, you will put them into either Category One, Two, or Three above. Just remember Do NOT Answer their call at this time.

Chapter Sixteen

Following the Script

You have sent Text #1, which starts either:

- *"Hey John, I just found out ..."*

- *"Hey John, I'm just curious ..."*

Remember you tweaked Text #1 based on your particular company, and this is what the prospect is replying to. Then continue with the script by:

Sending them Text #2 ... **"Ok, I have a very short video ... can you watch it right now?"**

This text will work for any company - no tweaking necessary! It is critical you keep the text as is. You're being positive and conveying a couple things to them.

- They will be committing to ONLY a few minutes.

- They need to be able to view it immediately.

The, *"right now,"* part is crucial and will save you from having to send annoying follow-ups, as I will demonstrate.

The prospect can respond in a couple of different ways. They can ignore you; in which case treat them in the same way as others who ignore your text - we will deal with them later. The prospect may respond and say they are driving, or not able to view your text at that moment. No problem!

Text Response: **"No problem, what would be a good time for you to watch the video?"**

We are allowing the prospect to think they are running the show. But since this is exactly how we run our business, we are still on script! Let's say the prospect responds with, *"tonight at 6pm."* You simply confirm, *"OK, I'll contact you then."*

Go on repeating this process until they commit to watching the video, "right now." Why is this so important? Because if they bug you to, *"Just send me the video and I'll watch it later today"* and you fall for it ... this is what will happen over the next day or week:

"Hey John, just checking to see if you watched the video yet"

"Hi there ... just checking in ... did you see it yet?"

"Hey ... it's me ... did you have time yet?

"Yo bud, did you see the video?"

"Checking in!"

"Hellooooooo!"

You have now succeeded in becoming that annoying friend they thought you might be when they originally responded. Because you put THEM in charge of YOUR business. Remember, nobody cares about your business as much as you do! That means YOU need to maintain control.

As long as you faithfully follow the script, your prospect will, either immediately or somewhere down the road, commit to watching your video, *"right now."* As soon as they do, you will send them:

Text #3. *"Great, here is the link (insert your video link here) ... I'll call you in 10 minutes."* Again, you are reiterating they need to watch the video right now and because you have told them you will be calling them in ten minutes, you've created a sense of urgency. Obviously, if you have a ten-minute video call them in 15 minutes. Basically, you want to give them a few minutes longer than the length of your video. Do NOT send a 30-minute webinar! Make sure it is a SHORT video. I suggest no longer than five or six minutes.

So far so good. You have done a great job as a recruiter!

1. You have stayed quiet!

2. You found a positive prospect.

3. You have the prospect watching your video

4. And your prospect is expecting your call in ten minutes!

Time to take action and let your Success Team, or Team Leaders, know you will have a three-way for them in about 12 minutes. The rule here is, however long the video is add two minutes and then another five minutes. So if your video is three minutes, add your two minutes and then another five - and you should be calling your Team Leader about ten minutes after your prospect begins watching the video. I know, your question now is, how can I guarantee the prospect will agree to the call with your Team Leader? (Spoiler Alert!) Follow the script … it leads them right there! Text, call, send smoke signals, whatever … just get a Team Leader alerted so you have someone to three-way with the prospect and yourself. This is why I mentioned earlier, how critical it is for you to have at least four to six up-line leaders on speed dial.

CHAPTER SEVENTEEN

Calling Your Prospect

YOU: Hi ____, thanks for taking a few minutes to check out that quick video ... I have a couple quick questions for you ... First off ... what did you like best?

FOCUS! You do NOT call up and start talking about the weather, sports, the kids, party plans for the weekend, work, or politics ... you FOCUS on the task at hand! You also don't ask them what they think. You steer the conversation to what they like *BEST* about the video, and that question will trigger the appropriate answer.

PROSPECT: "Yeah. I liked the _____ part."

YOU: "Yes, I saw that too when I watched the video."

Agree with the prospect here. Don't argue about what they liked best in the video. As long as they liked something you are still moving forward! The reality is, whatever they liked in the video you have seen that in the video too – providing, of course, you have watched your company's videos!

Now you immediately go into question two. This process is like, "taking the prospects' temperature." The last thing you want to do is over-sell someone who is ready to go or waste your time on someone who refuses to be open minded. When you ask the second question, you *MUST* wait for an answer. Do not speak again until the prospect gives you a number ... don't worry ... they will! I know a few seconds of silence can feel like forever, but you need to keep quiet so maintain the upper hand and control of YOUR business. Remember, *YOU* are steering this ship!

YOU: "Let me ask you, on a scale of one to ten ... one being ... I can't believe you made me watch that video! Ten being ... Sign me up! I'm ready to start right now!"

"Where would you place yourself on that scale?"

PROSPECT: Will give you a number. (Do NOT speak until he or she gives you a number!)

If that number is between eight and ten:

YOU: "That's about what I felt when I took a first look ... Since you're already near a computer (or smartphone) hop on my website and I'll show you just how simple the signup

process is and we'll have you set up in no time and then I'll introduce you to _____ who has been instrumental in my success, and they will help you as well.

(Three-way to team leader after sign-up for introduction)

If that number is between two and seven: (This is where 90% of your prospects will be, so get really good at this section).

YOU: "Ok ... That probably means you have a few questions. Tell me, what questions can I get addressed for you that would get you closer to a ten?"

(Typically a person will have two - four questions. Remember, you are NEW - You DON'T answer questions).

PROSPECT: Will give you their top questions.

YOU: "These are very good questions ... similar to mine as I got started ... as you know, I'm NEW, but there is someone I work directly with _____, who is an amazing team leader. He/she has done such an amazing job supporting me and has been instrumental in my growing success. He/she is very familiar with all the ins and outs of the business and would be perfect to address your questions ... Hold on a minute!"

Your team leaders should have been alerted that you have a prospect. Three-way directly to them immediately ... Do NOT ask for permission! This is YOUR business!

You want both parties to feel good going into their conversation so practice talking nicely about your team leaders and potential prospects. If you aren't sure, ask you ask your TL to assist you in learning how to properly edify people.

YOU: (EDIFY TEAM LEADER). "Hi _____ (TL), thank you so much fortaking my call on short notice! As you know, I'm still new to thisbusiness and I was just telling _____ (prospect) howknowledgeable and helpful you have been to me in starting mynew business." (EDIFY PROSPECT) "I've known _____ (prospect)for x long. _____ prospect) is a business person; they've donethis, that, and the other thing :-)"

YOU: _____, (TL) _____(prospect) watched our video, rated themselves a #, and has some great questions. I knew you would be the best person to address them! So with that I'll turn the call over to you."

At this point the team leader will take over the call and you will hit MUTE! Yes, I mean it ... hit the mute button on your phone.

The team leader will conduct the call from this point and you are NOT to interrupt for any reason. Doing so will DE-EDIFY your leader!

Your job, here is to listen ... Learn ... Take notes ... Even if you've heard it 104 times this week! Once your Team Leader has addressed all of your prospects initial questions and probably a few follow up ones they will move to what I like to refer to as the "softest close in the industry"!

TL: Well, _____, (prospect) I believe we have addressed most, if not all of your questions and at this point I have one simple question for you? You were at # when we started this conversation ... so at this point, how much closer to a ten do you see yourself?

Based on the number your prospect provides as their new number, your direction with them will become clear.

If the prospect has moved up to the eight to ten range, the team leader will turn them back over to you so you can sign them up and get them started on the path to building their own business alongside you. They can start later that same day by using the Shut & Text system, which you will no doubt share with them!

If the prospect indicates they are still a seven or less, then your TL will recommend a couple videos, a webinar, a local meeting, an additional three-way call, etc. This is also the time to schedule another call to review the information the prospect will be looking at.

For example:

TL: "OK, _____ (prospect), you began rating your interest as a four and now you are rating yourself a six, which typically means you would like to review some additional information before making your final decision. We have a few videos on our YouTube channel that you can review and please write down any additional questions that come to mind. Quick question, how much time will it take you to review a few three to five minute videos?"

(Prospect answers)

TL: "Great. As my schedule gets a bit crazy, let's make an appointment for that evening. What works best for you. 7.00pm or 9.00pm?"

(Always allow the prospect to choose from a couple of different times; it gives them the illusion of being in control).

TL: "OK ... I'll turn you back over to _____ (you), and I look forward to touching base with you again at the time you chose. You're in very capable hands ... Goodbye for now."

Once the three-way call is over, the TL will turn the prospect back over to you and at this point you thank your TL and remind your prospect that the TL will also be there for them when they begin to build their business, because it's all part of the great support your incredible team offers!

Inevitably, your list will start to get a bit messy, but that's OK. Below is just a sample of some of the information you'll be recording. BE ACCURATE! Use a highlighter if you need to follow up , put it on your calendar and set an alarm in your phone. I also suggest texting your team leader on the day of the call to remind them. Your TL is busy so be proactive and they will really appreciate it!

Joe Smith – T1 (4/15 @ 2:30pm)

~~Mary Jo~~ T1 (4/15 @ 2:30pm) – T2 (4/15 @ 2:45) – T3 (4/15 @ 2:45) … Called @ 2:50 … 3way with Don … Signing up ~~Chucky Jones~~ NOT Bobby D – T1 (4/15 @ 2:30pm) – T2 (4/16 @ 10am) … NA … Contact 4/16 @ 3pm

Ira Goldberg – T1 (4/15 @ 2:30pm) – T2 (4/15 @ 7:45) – T3 (4/15 @ 7:45) … Called @ 7:50 … 3way with Don … Said NO … agree to be added to update list.

Bill Smith – T1 (4/15 @ 2:30pm) … SR … (means - snarky response)

CHAPTER EIGHTEEN

The Decision!

Most people have heard the saying - The money is in the follow up, the money is in the follow up, the money is in the follow up ...

UGH!!! I want to scream every time I hear that! I'm not saying don't follow up, but I will say there is NO money in following up. WHAT? I know that will sound sacrilegious to some people, but give me a minute to help you understand what I mean.

Think about this: (Take notes ... it's IMPORTANT!)

If your prospect says, "yes," then you say, "Great, let's get you signed up. I'll show you where the training information is located. We'll order you a copy of *'Shut Up & Text ,'* (shameless plug!) I'll introduce you to some of our team leaders and get you started making money ASAP."

If your prospect says "I'm not sure," you set a follow up for, say a week. Again, your prospect isn't sure so you set a follow up for a month. Your prospect is still undecided so you follow up in another month and so on and so on ... HOW MUCH MONEY ARE YOU MAKING WITH THEM? Compared to the time you are spending? ZERO!

If your prospect says, "no," then you say, "OK, I want to thank you so much for taking the time to review the information as it meant a lot to me. But, as you have realized by now, I'm really excited about this company and I plan to make a serious run with them. Would you mind if I kept you updated as to my progress with them over the coming months?"

Because you have acted in a professional manner, you will find most people will be pleasantly surprised and over 90% will readily agree to receiving updates from you. This is great news but you need to NOT abuse this privilege. If you do this properly, people will come back asking to join you down the road.

Your updates should be SHORT – I mean EXTREMELY short and to the point. If you write them a novel, folk will simply hit the DELETE key - and that doesn't make you money! Use a simple mail program such as Constant Contact, Mailchimp or similar and personalize your updates so it looks like you are

ONLY going to and speaking to them! Remember, keep your updates informative but ... SHORT!

Here are a couple of examples:

"Hey {First Name} I just wanted to let you know that I've attained a new rank within _____ (company) which, of course comes with a pay increase! Some exciting news is breaking soon and I can't wait. Thank you for your support, Sign

Hey {First Name} _____ (company) just came out with a new product ... it tastes great and is helping me lose weight while I make money. Onward and upward! Thank you for your support, Sign

Hey {First Name} Wow! As you know; I've been working my tail off with _____ (company). Very excited to announce I'm one of their contest winners and will be off to Cancun in March!! Thank you for your support, Sign

It's extremely important you keep the updates short and to the point. Be as upbeat and informative as possible. Finally, always and I mean always, thank them for their support. This allows you to constantly update everyone who has said, "no." By using a mail system, you can fully update ALL of them in the same time it would have taken for you to update ONE person!

For many people, it is simply not a good time for them to join you in your business or some may not believe you will stick with it, so they want to know you are serious before they commit. By keeping the updates professional, regular, informative and upbeat, down the road as their situation changes, your name will come to mind. Situations that affect people's outlook on a home-based business are:

- Laid off at work

- Spouse laid off

- Little to NO raise again this year

- Tired of the place where they work

- Stay at home mom now has the kids in school half day

- Stock market downturn

- Retirement isn't all it's cracked up to be (boredom!)

- Current network marketing company not living up to expectations

- Wanting to pay off debt sooner

Don't worry about trying to figure out why someone on your, "no," list will come back to you and be ready to engage. That isn't your job. Your job is to keep them informed so that when the time is right they will know that YOU are the person they need to talk with about fixing their situation. When they call, try to keep the initial chat brief, assess why they are calling and what they are looking for to help their current situation. That means you do a lot of LISTENING not talking! Once you have figured out what the reasons are, you let the prospect know you, "may have a SOLUTION for them." Not that you have a business; not that you have the answer to their prayers; no hype ... keep it real. Then revert immediately to the script (Text #2) ... **"I have a very short video; can you watch it right now?"**

It's important for your success that you move them right into the script. This is what you will be teaching them when helping them launch their own business in the next few days, so don't handicap them by talking for hours and explaining everything like you now know you are NOT supposed to do! Remember to ... Shut Up!

Important takeaway from this section!

The MONEY is in the DECISION!

I really like the sign a friend of mine keeps near his computer. (You may want to steal this from him - like I did!)

Give me YES, give me a NO, I gotta GO!!

CHAPTER NINETEEN

Fun and Following Up

W ant to have some fun?

Remember all those people you texted who ignored you or sent you a snarky response? I mentioned it earlier, but it's important to review since many of these folks will come around at some point in the future, you never know, but let's review and have some fun with them!

It's important to understand that they saw your text. They read it, they're choosing to ignore you. I know this annoys many of you because some of you have made excuses like; they didn't see it or they must be really busy. Face it! They may not have seen it right away, but they saw it and the reason you know they saw it is human nature - everybody gets a little red circle on their messages icon with a number in it. When you get a little red circle and it says you have a text, do you leave that circle for days? Do you even leave it for hours? Minutes? NO! You read every single text that comes through, or you at least glance at it. Guess what? Your friends do too! If they didn't answer you, it's because they chose not to. That's okay, because you don't know what their situation is. What if …

- They had a terrible day at work.

- They had a fight with their boyfriend/girlfriend.

- They had a fight with their spouse.

- Pet died.

- Car crash.

- Kids sick.

- Parent fell and broke hip.

- Moving.

- Traveling for work/vacation.

- Dropped phone in a pool (yes, I've done this!).

So now we have given them every excuse in the book, let's realize the majority just ignored you for no good reason! I know, it's annoying! But we must be sensible if we want a possible future working relationship with them. Act like a professional!

That doesn't mean we can't have some fun with it though! Here's how I handle them - I go back to the people who didn't answer me maybe one or two weeks later, and I text them. These are some actual examples:

(PWIM = Prospect Who Ignored Me! the nerve of some people!)

ME: "Are you okay?"

PWIM: "Yeah, I'm okay why?"

ME: "Well, you ignored my text last week, and I figured something may have been wrong so I gave you a bit of time."

PWIM: "What text?"

Now I have them right where I want them. The conversation is started and I revert right back to the original Text #1

If they ignore the, "Are you OK," text, I give them about a week and then I text them again:

ME: "Did you fall in a hole?"

If they still don't respond, I wait at least another week and then text them:

ME: "Hope you're ok ... Do I need to send flowers?"

If they still don't respond, I wait at least another week and text them:

ME: "Jeez you must have died ... where do I send flowers?"

If they still don't respond I wait at least another week and text them:

ME: "OK, I've sent you a number of texts over the last month or so and I've heard crickets. If I don't hear back from you I will close the file on you."

I've only needed the ultimate, "close the file on you," with a few people as usually one of the other texts gets them to respond. It's important to remember you are not here to get into an argument. No matter how they respond, you are to simply let them know you sent them a couple texts and didn't hear back. Then revert to the texting script with Text #1. This becomes a habit and will make your life so much simpler and anyone who joins your business will be mostly trained on how to prospect by the time they join!

Now, some people may be having a bad day and they're going to send you an obnoxious text; it might be an ignorant one, it might be a stupid one. It might be an attempt to get you into a fight because they're in a bad mood. The point is, it doesn't matter what they send you ... YOU remain professional!

Here are some of the snarky texts I've received; keep a list of yours and we can compare some day!

- Are you doing one of those pyramids?

- What are you doing now?

- Getting rich?

- Did you take over the world yet?

- I can't believe you are still doing those things!

- OMG ... really?

- Why don't you get a real job?

- Walmart is hiring.

- Did you buy that island yet?

These are extremely annoying people and your job is to ignore them! I know it's tough sometimes because you want to get into a texting or messaging war with them and show them just how stupid they are and how smart you are! You can put them in their place in ten minutes and you know it! You will show them ... **NOT!!!**

Don't do it! WHY? Because if you do, it will be a temporary victory and then you will realize that war made you no money and destroyed that prospect for life. Remember, for most people it is just not the right time in their life to get involved in a home-based business. Also remember ... eventually their situation will change as it does with every human on the planet. Stay professional and you will be rewarded down the road.

Once they engage ... go back to Text #1 and follow the script until they say yes and join your team, or say no and go on the update list.

Do you want to know why these follow up texts work? Because they get people's attention. They go **"HEY, I'm talking to you!"** They make people pay attention to you. You *are* going to answer me! I don't care if anybody says, "no," to my business, but I do care if they disrespect me. If you ignore me, we're no longer going to be friends. When I "close the file" on someone, I literally delete that person out of my phone. Gone, gone, don't even call me again - ever. I don't want to know you. That sounds harsh, doesn't it? Yeah, but why would you put up with disrespectful people in your life?

You need to remember it is YOUR business and you are not asking or begging people to join or to spend money with you. You are asking them to have respect and to take at least a quick look at a short video. If your friends or acquaintances don't respect you enough to watch a three to five-minute video and say "no," then you need some new friends. (Yeah, I have replaced many over the years! ... and so will you as your grow your business)

Be willing to be tough. You need to have the attitude ... I have 5,000 people on FB, and over 4,200 in my phone. Do you think I'm going to miss a few?

It rarely gets to that point, because the texts are obnoxious enough to get their attention and they usually answer. Again, do I care whether they say yes or no? The only thing I care about is if you take the time to do me a favor and look at something for a few minutes. That's all I ask because if you can't do that, we don't need to be friends. You see, this is why I demand respect if we're friends.

What that means to me is, if you call me when you're stuck on the side of the road, I don't whine, bitch, moan, groan, complain or make any excuses. I simply ask one question: Where are you? So, if I'm willing to do that for my friends and acquaintances, then asking them to sit wherever they are comfy for a short while and watch a three to five minute video, is EXTREMELY reasonable in my book!

Chapter Twenty

"It Doesn't Hurt!"

I f you want to make six figures or move up to seven figures in network marketing, you need to love the word, "NO!" Seriously, it doesn't hurt. The difference between someone who makes $100/month and someone who earn $10,000/month is the number of No's they have heard! You want to go higher than that in income? Go for 1,000 NO's or how about 5,000?

Remember, people are not saying NO to you. They are saying NO to the opportunity you are sharing with them. Think about this ... When you decided to start your business who made that decision? RIGHT ... YOU made that decision! That means you must have respect for people, share a concept with them and if they see what you do and make a decision to start a business as well, then you will be working together.

It's important that your prospect makes their OWN decision to go into business with you. Because if you SELL them or convince them, to go into business with you, then you have a huge uphill battle in front of you. You will need to convince them to set goals. Then convince them to do a vision board. Then convince them to make a list. Then convince them to start texting, etc. It's going to be a constant sell job for you ... so NO convincing ... simply share!

If you are like me and despise wasting time, make sure your prospects are on the same page as you and they want to build a business. It's about duplication! You can't duplicate quickly if you're wasting time constantly convincing people.

CHAPTER TWENTY-ONE

What To Do Right Now!

This *Shut Up & Text* system was developed to remove negativity and increase duplication, thereby increasing the speed of building your way to 100k!

In closing, I am going to blow another famous saying out of the water ... are you ready?

"Slow and steady wins the race." Blah! Not true! And don't give me the tortoise and the hare story! The only reason the hare lost is that he went to sleep!

Business growth loves speed. All out massive action over a sustained period of time, will get you the results you desire.

For fastest results share your new knowledge of the Shut Up & Text system with your team and your team leaders and join our WWKM tribe!

So ... ARE YOU READY?

Then what are you waiting for ... get BUILDING ... much success is awaiting you and your team!

I will be here for you ... please feel free to reach out as I work with people from all over the world on a weekly basis.

For continued personal development, growth and training, join the WWKM Tribe and follow me at ...

FB ... Facebook.com/WorkWithKevinMarino

FB Group ... facebook.com/groups/WWKMChallenge

FB Messenger ... KevinMarinoCT

Instagram ... search @Work_With_KevinMarino

www.InstaGram.com/Work_With_KevinMarino

www.WorkWithKevinMarino.com

I speak at many events around the country. When you see me, please come up and introduce yourself as I truly love meeting new folks ... especially budding entrepreneurs and network marketers!